My First Animal Library

Zebras

by Cari Meister

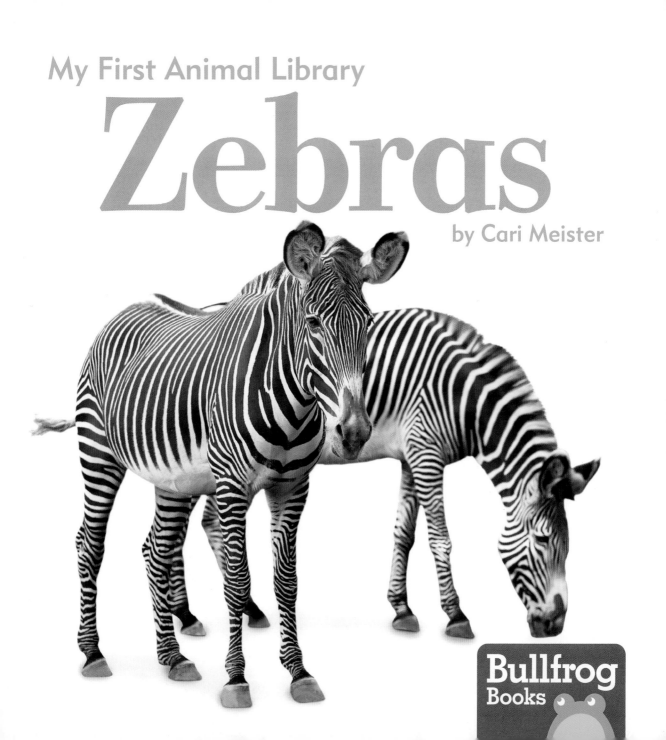

Bullfrog Books

Ideas for Parents and Teachers

Bullfrog Books let children practice reading informational text at the earliest reading levels. Repetition, familiar words, and photo labels support early readers.

Before Reading

- Discuss the cover photo. What does it tell them?
- Look at the picture glossary together. Read and discuss the words.

Read the Book

- "Walk" through the book and look at the photos. Let the child ask questions. Point out the photo labels.
- Read the book to the child, or have him or her read independently.

After Reading

- Prompt the child to think more. Ask: Have you seen a zebra before? Do you think zebras are white with black stripes? Or are they black with white stripes?

Bullfrog Books are published by Jump!
5357 Penn Avenue South
Minneapolis, MN 55419
www.jumplibrary.com

Library of Congress Cataloging-in-Publication Data

Meister, Cari, author.
 Zebras/by Cari Meister.
    pages cm.—(Bullfrog books.
My first animal library)
 Audience: Ages 5.
 Audience: K to grade 3.
 Includes index.
 ISBN 978-1-62031-171-4 (hardcover)
 ISBN 978-1-62496-258-5 (ebook)
 1. Zebras—Juvenile literature. I. Title.
QL737.U62M45 2015
599.665'7—dc23
                                              2014032154

Series Editor: Wendy Dieker
Series Designer: Ellen Huber
Book Designer: Lindaanne Donohoe
Photo Researcher: Jenny Fretland VanVoorst

Photo Credits: All photos by Shutterstock except: Alamy, 12; Corbis, 19; National Geographic Creative, 16–17; SuperStock, 8–9, 14–15, 23tr, 23br; Thinkstock, cover.

Printed in the United States of America at Corporate Graphics in North Mankato, Minnesota.

Table of Contents

On the Lookout

It is hot.

A zebra herd goes to the water hole.

They drink.

A zebra stands guard.
Is danger near?

No. No danger now.

The zebras swish
their tails.

The bugs stay away.

The foals don't drink water.

They drink mama's milk.

foal

Some zebras kick.

They fight for space.

12

The guard watches.

A lion stalks.

She is the color of weeds.

The zebras do not see her.

The lion runs.

She chases.

Run, zebra! Run!

Zebras have hard hooves.

hoof

They kick at the lion.

The lion runs away.

The herd is safe for now.

21

Parts of a Zebra

ears
Zebras have large ears; they can hear very well.

stripes
No two zebras have the same stripes.

eyes
Zebras have large eyes and can see very well.

Picture Glossary

foal
A baby zebra.

stalk
To hunt an animal in a quiet, careful way.

herd
A group of zebras that live together.

swish
To swing back and forth.

Index

To Learn More

Learning more is as easy as 1, 2, 3.

1) Go to www.factsurfer.com

2) Enter "zebras" into the search box.

3) Click the "Surf" button to see a list of websites.

With factsurfer.com, finding more information is just a click away.